Witness at the Cross
Leader Guide

Witness at the Cross
A Beginner's Guide to Holy Friday

Witness at the Cross
978-1-7910-2112-2
978-1-7910-2113-9 *eBook*

Witness at the Cross DVD
978-1-7910-2122-1

Witness at the Cross Leader Guide
978-1-7910-2114-6
978-1-7910-2115-3 *eBook*

Also by Amy-Jill Levine

Entering the Passion of Jesus
A Beginner's Guide to Holy Week

Light of the World
A Beginner's Guide to Advent

Sermon on the Mount
A Beginner's Guide to the Kingdom of Heaven

The Difficult Words of Jesus
A Beginner's Guide to His Most Perplexing Teachings

AMY-JILL LEVINE

WITNESS
at the CROSS

A BEGINNER'S GUIDE *to* HOLY FRIDAY

LEADER GUIDE

by Mike S. Poteet

Abingdon Press | Nashville

Witness at the Cross:
A Beginner's Guide to Holy Friday
Leader Guide

978-1-7910-2114-6

21 22 23 24 25 26 27 28 29 30 — 10 9 8 7 6 5 4 3 2 1
MANUFACTURED IN THE UNITED STATES OF AMERICA

CONTENTS

AMPLIFY
MEDIA

Watch videos based on *Witness at the Cross:
A Beginner's Guide to Holy Friday* with Amy-Jill Levine
through Amplify Media.

Amplify Media is a multimedia platform that delivers
high quality, searchable content with an emphasis
on Wesleyan perspectives for churchwide, group,
or individual use on any device at any time. In a
world of sometimes overwhelming choices, ***Amplify
Media*** gives church leaders and congregants media
capabilities that are contemporary, relevant, effective
and, most importantly, affordable and sustainable.

With ***Amplify Media*** church leaders can:
- Provide a reliable source of Christian content
  through a Wesleyan lens for teaching, training, and
  inspiration in a customizable library,
- Deliver their own preaching and worship content in
  a way your congregation knows and appreciates,
- Build the church's capacity to innovate with
  engaging content and accessible technology,
- Equip the congregation to better understand the
  Bible and its application, and
- Deepen discipleship beyond the church walls.

Ask your group leader or pastor about Amplify
Media and sign up today at **AmplifyMedia.com**.

INTRODUCTION

In *Witness at the Cross*, Dr. Amy-Jill Levine (she prefers to be called "AJ") offers readers an uncommon and fascinating approach to studying the Gospel accounts of Jesus's crucifixion.

Rather than focusing immediately and directly on Jesus—as much Christian preaching, liturgy, and devotion do—AJ invites readers to see the Crucifixion and consider anew its significance through the eyes and ears of those who watched it happen and heard what was said by Jesus and those around him, according to the four New Testament Gospels.

When we consider Jesus's death from these people's unique and diverse points of view, we may well discover it means not less but even more than Christians often consider. AJ's approach allows readers to experience in fresh and frequently surprising ways the Crucifixion's power to shake preconceptions about who we are, who God is, and the shape our life in God's presence takes.

This Leader Guide is designed to help people involved in adult education programs in a congregational setting to facilitate a six-session study of AJ's book. While this guide includes substantial quotations from *Witness at the Cross*, it doesn't cover everything the book does and presupposes (as AJ would point out, perhaps optimistically) participants will be reading the book as part of their study.

Here is a "sneak peek" at topics covered in these session plans:

- **Session 1** lets participants "listen in" on the derision those standing by the cross, including some of Jerusalem's political leaders, the chief priests and scribes, hurled at Jesus as he died. What do their words show us about the nature of blasphemy, and how does their presence force us to confront our own complicity: Can bystanders be innocent?

- **Session 2** brings participants closer to the closest witnesses of Jesus's death: the two men crucified alongside him. How do their deaths at the hands of Rome's judicial system both challenge our views of criminal justice today and move us to live as good neighbors to our fellow human beings?

- **Session 3** introduces participants to the Roman soldiers at the cross and the centurion who commanded them. To what extent does those soldiers' apparent indifference to Jesus's death indict us as we go about our business while innocents die—and, in contrast, to what extent can we make the centurion's profession of respect and awe as Jesus dies our own?

- **Session 4** considers the role of the Beloved Disciple in the Fourth Gospel's story of Jesus's ministry and death. What can this anonymous but important figure teach participants about Jesus's "new command" to love each other and about observing all our time as sacred time?

- **Session 5** examines the place of the women who followed Jesus, served as his patrons, and supported him at his cross; by extension, the chapter therefore examines the place and role of women in churches today. AJ points out not only the different roles the women at the cross play, she asks what roles women and men can play in bearing witness to God and Jesus in powerful ways.

- **Session 6** asks how Joseph of Arimathea and Nicodemus related to Jesus before he died and why their actions in burying his body provide a model for modern "sympathizers" of Jesus. It also asks participants how their encounters with the witnesses at the cross have influenced their own faith and practice.

You probably will not have time to address all the questions this guide suggests. Regard the contents as prompts to help your discussion flow and to dive deeper into topics participants find interesting or compelling.

Leading Virtual Small-Group Sessions

Meeting online is a great option for a number of situations. During the time of a public-health hazard, such as the COVID-19 pandemic, online meetings are a welcome opportunity for people to converse while seeing each other's faces. Online meetings can also expand the "neighborhood" of possible group members, because people can log in from just about anywhere in the world. This online gathering also gives those who do not have access to transportation or who prefer not to travel at certain times of day the chance to participate.

The guidelines below will help you lead an effective and enriching group study using an online video conferencing platform such as Zoom, Webex, Google Meet, Microsoft Teams, or other virtual meeting platform of your choice.

Basic Features for Virtual Meetings

There are many choices for videoconferencing platforms. You may have personal experience and comfort using a particular service, or your church may have a subscription that will influence your choice. Whichever option you choose, it is recommended that you use a platform that supports the following features:

- **Synchronous video and audio:** Your participants can see and speak to each other live, in real time. Participants have the ability to turn their video off and on, and to mute and unmute their audio.

- **Chat:** Your participants can send text messages to the whole group or individuals from within the virtual meeting. Participants can put active hyperlinks (i.e., "clickable" internet addresses) into the chat for other participants' convenience.

- **Screen Sharing:** Participants can share the contents of their screen with other participants (the meeting host's permission may be required).

- **Video Sharing:** Participants (or the host) can share videos and computer audio via screen share, so that all participants can view the videos each week.

- **Breakout Rooms:** Meeting hosts can automatically or manually send participants into virtual smaller groups, and they can determine whether or not participants will return to the main group automatically after a set period of time. Hosts can communicate with all breakout rooms. This feature is useful if your group is large or if you wish to break into smaller teams of two or three for certain activities. If you have a smaller group, this feature may not be necessary.

Check with your clergy or director of discipleship to see if your church has a preferred platform or an account with one or more of these platforms that you might use. In most instances, only the host will need to be signed in to the account; others can participate without being registered.

Zoom, Webex, Google Meet, and Microsoft Teams all offer free versions of their platform, which you can use if your church doesn't have an account. However, there may be some restrictions (for instance, Zoom's free version limits meetings to 45 minutes). Check each platform's website to be sure you are aware of any such restrictions before you sign up.

Once you have selected a platform, familiarize yourself with all of its features and controls so that you can facilitate virtual meetings comfortably. The platform's website will have lists of features and helpful tutorials, and often third-party sites will have useful information or instructions as well.

In addition to videoconferencing software, it is also advisable to have access to slide-creation software such as Microsoft PowerPoint or Google Slides. These can be used to prepare easy slides for screen-sharing to display discussion questions, quotes from the study book, or Scripture passages. If you don't have easy access to these, you can create a document and share it—but make sure the print size is easy to read.

Video Sharing

For a video-based study, it's important to be able to screen-share your videos so that all participants can view them in your study session. The good news is, whether you have the videos on DVD or streaming files, it is possible to play them in your session.

All of the videoconferencing platforms mentioned above support screen-sharing videos. Some have specific requirements for assuring that sound will play clearly in addition to the videos. Follow your videoconferencing platform instructions carefully and test the video sharing in advance to be sure it works.

If you wish to screen-share a DVD video, you may need to use a different media player. Some media players will not allow you to share your screen when you play copyright-protected DVDs. VLC is a free media player that is safe and easy to use. To try this software, download at videolan.org/VLC.

What about copyright? DVDs like those you use for group study are meant to be used in a group setting "real time." That is, whether you meet in person, online, or in a hybrid setting, Abingdon Press encourages use of your DVD or streaming video.

What is allowed: Streaming an Abingdon DVD over Zoom, Teams, or similar platform during a small group session.

What is not allowed: Posting video of a published DVD study to social media or YouTube for later viewing.

If you have any questions about permissions and copyright, email permissions@abingdonpress.com.

Amplify Media. The streaming subscription platform Amplify Media makes it easy to share streaming videos for groups. When your church has an Amplify subscription, your group members can sign on and have access to the video sessions. With access, they may watch the video on their own ahead of your group meeting, watch the streaming video during your group meeting, or view again after the meeting. Thousands of videos are on AmplifyMedia.com making it easy to watch anytime, anywhere, and on any device from phones and tablets to Smart TVs and desktops.

Visit AmplifyMedia.com to learn more or call 1-800-672-1789, option 4, to hear about the current offers.

Communicating with Your Group

Clear communication with your small group before and throughout your study is crucial no matter how you meet, but it is doubly important if you are gathering virtually.

Advertising the Study. Be sure to advertise your virtual study on your church's website and/or in its newsletter, as well as any social media that your church uses. Request that pastors or other worship leaders announce it in worship services.

Registration. Encourage people to register for the online study so that you can know all participants and have a way to contact them. Ideally, you will collect an email address for each participant so that you can send them communications and links to your virtual meeting sessions. An event planning tool such as SignUpGenius makes this easy, and it gives you a database of participants and their email addresses.

Welcome Email. Before your first session, several days in advance, send an email to everyone who has registered for the study, welcoming them to the group, reminding them of the date and time of your first meeting, and including a link to join the virtual meeting.

It's also a good idea to include one or two discussion questions to "prime the pump" for reflection and conversation when you gather.

If you have members without internet service, or if they are uncomfortable using a computer and videoconferencing software, let them know they may telephone into the meeting. Provide them the number and let them know that there is usually a unique phone number for each meeting.

Weekly Emails. Send a new email two or three days before each week's session, again including the link to join your virtual meeting and one or two discussion questions to set the stage for discussion. Feel free to use any of the questions in the Leader Guide for this purpose. If you find a particular quote from the book that is especially meaningful, include this as well.

Facebook. Consider creating a private Facebook group for your small group. Here you can both hold discussion and invite reflection between your weekly meetings. Each week, post one or two quotes from the study book along with a short question for reflection and invite people to respond in the comments. These questions can come straight from the Leader Guide, and you can revisit the Facebook conversation during your virtual meeting.

You might also consider posting these quotes and questions on your church's main Facebook page, inviting people in your congregation to join the conversation beyond your small group. This can be a great way to involve others in your study, or to let people know about it and invite them to join your next virtual meeting.

During Your Virtual Sessions

During your virtual sessions, follow these tips to be sure you are prepared and that everything runs as smoothly as possible.

- Familiarize yourself with the controls and features of your videoconferencing platform, using instructions or tutorials available via the platform's website or third-party sites.

- Be sure you are leading the session from a well-lit place in front of a background free from excessive distractions.
- As leader, log into the virtual meeting early. You want to be a good host who is present to welcome participants by name as they arrive. This also gives you time to check how you appear on camera, so that you can make any last-minute adjustments to your lighting and background if needed.
- During each session, pay attention to who is speaking and who is not. Because of video and audio lags as well as internet connections of varying quality, some participants may inadvertently speak over each other without realizing they are doing so. As needed, directly prompt specific people to speak if they wish (for example, "Alan, it looked like you were about to say something when Sarah was speaking").
- If your group is especially large, you may want to agree with members on a procedure for being recognized to speak (for example, participants might "raise hands" digitally or type "call on me" in the chat feature).
- Instruct participants to keep their microphones muted during the meeting, so extraneous noise from their location does not interrupt the meeting. This includes chewing or yawning sounds, which can be embarrassing! When it is time for discussion, participants can unmute themselves.
- Remember, some participants may wish simply to observe and listen—do not pressure anyone to speak who does not wish to.
- Always get your group's permission before recording your online sessions. While those who are unable to attend the meeting may appreciate the chance to view it later, respect the privacy of your participants.

In challenging times, modern technology has powerful potential to bring God's people together in new and nourishing ways. May such be your experience during this virtual study.

Session 1

BYSTANDERS AND SCOFFERS

Session Goals

This session's readings and discussion will help participants:

- Use the passersby's and political leaders' derision of Jesus as a lens through which to think about what constitutes blasphemy.
- Explore Jesus's and Christianity's relationship to the Jerusalem Temple, as well as modern Christians' relationship to the places where they worship.
- Consider the continuing significance of the inscription on Jesus's cross.
- Identify situations of wrongdoing in which they will avoid becoming not-so-innocent bystanders.

Biblical Foundations

Those who passed by derided Jesus, shaking their heads and saying, "Aha! You who would destroy the temple and build it in three days, save yourself, and come down from the cross!" In the same way the chief priests, along with the scribes, were also mocking him among themselves and saying, "He saved others; he cannot save himself. Let the Messiah, the King of Israel, come down from the cross now, so that we may see and believe." Those who were crucified with him also taunted him.

Mark 15:29-32

Pilate also had an inscription written and put on the cross. It read, "Jesus of Nazareth, the King of the Jews." Many of the Jews read this inscription, because the place where Jesus was crucified was near the city; and it was written in Hebrew, in Latin, and in Greek. Then the chief priests of the Jews said to Pilate, "Do not write, 'The King of the Jews,' but, 'This man said, I am King of the Jews.'" Pilate answered, "What I have written I have written."

John 19:19-22

Before Your Session

- Read the introduction and chapter 1 of *Witness at the Cross*, noting topics about which you want or need to do further research.

- Read this session's Biblical Foundations several times, as well as background information about them from trusted biblical commentaries and other references.

- You will need: Bibles for participants and/or on-screen slides to share prepared with Biblical Foundations, newsprint, and a markerboard.

- *Optional:* Select an image of the Crucifixion (the first of the eventual six), preferably one that depicts bystanders watching the event.

Starting Your Session

Welcome participants. Begin by considering the material in the book's introduction, the overview of material, and discussion of Simon of Cyrene.

- Before you saw the list of chapters in the table of contents, who did you think would be included as witnesses at the cross? Why?

- Who is Simon of Cyrene, and what role does he play in the Crucifixion?

- Do you see Simon of Cyrene as complicit in Jesus's death? What does it mean that he bears the cross for Jesus?
- Is Simon also a victim? Why? How do you understand his role as a witness at the cross?

Optional: Add the first of the six images of the Crucifixion you've selected to the display in your meeting space, and/or share the image on your screen. Ask:

- What about this image most draws your attention, and why?
- (*If applicable*) Focus on this image's depiction of the bystanders. What thoughts and feelings does this aspect of the image evoke in you?
- What do you like about this image? What do you dislike about it?

Tell participants this session will explore how bystanders and passersby reacted to the Crucifixion.

Lead this prayer aloud or one of your own:

Holy God, strengthen us to stand, in our minds and hearts, before the cross of Jesus, that we may discover where you would have us stand and what you would have us say as his followers today. Amen.

Bystanders and Blasphemy

Recruit a volunteer to read aloud Mark 15:27-32. Discuss:

- Mark (and Matthew) describe passersby mocking Jesus. When, if ever, have you seen someone being publicly insulted, ridiculed, or shamed by a crowd? How did you respond?
- Mark says the chief priests and scribes (experts in biblical law)—and Matthew adds "elders" (27:41)—also mocked Jesus. In AJ's words, these leaders "would not be the first or the last representatives of a religious institution to be guilty

of hypocrisy." How do you respond when religious leaders fail to live up to the standards they represent? Do you think clergy or politicians should be held to a higher moral standard than laity?

- Mark and Matthew literally say the passersby "blasphemed" Jesus. AJ writes: "While the [Greek] term primarily means to 'abuse verbally,' the connotation of blasphemy, an offense against God, is not inappropriate." Why not?

- How would you answer AJ's question: "Can we recognize blasphemy when we hear it?" If we do hear it or see it, what should be our response? Are there certain words that should never be said?

- AJ notes that their taunts reveal a limited understanding of what it means to be "saved." Salvation can be a physical rescue; thus, it is not restricted to the divine; "saving is something we can do." Further, "in the Gospels, salvation . . . is also the state of a right relationship between humanity and divinity." To what extent is an understanding of salvation that neglects any of these aspects blasphemous? Why or why not?

- AJ asks, "Should there be laws against blasphemy?" What do you think, and why?

- In Luke 23:35, *only* the people's leaders "scoff" at Jesus; the people simply "watch." AJ wonders to what extent a people and its leaders should be differentiated, especially "in a participatory democracy wherein leaders are elected." How would you answer, and why?

Jesus and the Temple

Lead participants in brainstorming a list of everything the group knows about the Jerusalem Temple (about which the bystanders in Mark 15 and Matthew 27 taunt Jesus). Write responses on newsprint or markerboard or type them using your videoconferencing platform's whiteboard feature (if available). Encourage participants to think of and look up (using a Bible reference as needed) other Bible stories they may remember about the Temple. Don't be reluctant to "prime the pump" with some basic questions:"Where was it?" "Who built it?" "Who was worshipped there?" When done brainstorming, add any of the following information lacking from the list:

- King Solomon oversaw the first Temple's construction in Jerusalem in 957 BCE (1 Kings 6–8).
- The Babylonian Empire destroyed Solomon's Temple when it conquered Jerusalem in 587/586 BCE (2 Kings 25:8-10).
- The Jews who returned from the Babylonian Exile started building the second Temple in 538 BCE. King Herod the Great (the Herod of the "Christmas story" in Matthew 2) substantially renovated and rebuilt it, states AJ, "with the renovations continuing through the first half of the first century" (see John 2:20).
- The Roman army destroyed the second Temple in 70 CE. (The four New Testament Gospels were written after the Temple's destruction.)
- Today, the Dome of the Rock, an important Islamic monument, stands on the site of the first and second Temples.

Discuss:

- "While God was everywhere and so could be worshipped everywhere," AJ writes, "the Temple had [for most of the Jewish population] a special sanctity because it was God's house" (see Luke 2:49 and John 2:16) and "a symbol of the nation." How does this information help us understand the bystanders' derision of Jesus in Mark 15:29-30 and Matthew 27:39-40? What religious and/or political sites in your nation or in the world hold a Temple-like significance, and why? Do you think that a place can be holy, or is it the people who were and are there who make it holy?

- Read Mark 14:55-59 and Matthew 26:59-61. How accurate is the bystanders' information about Jesus and the Temple? What might their derision of Jesus suggest about the relationship between misinformation and hateful speech and action?
- Read John 2:13-22. What is Jesus's attitude toward the Temple in this story? How does it relate to Psalm 69:9? How does John interpret Jesus's words about destroying the Temple?
- AJ points out that as Christianity became a predominantly non-Jewish movement, its "original concerns for the Temple, Jerusalem, and the land of Israel" faded. To what or whom do 2 Corinthians 6:16 and Hebrews 9:24-28 relocate the Temple's significance? How do Christians today accept helpful aspects of these reinterpretations of the Temple while rejecting anti-Jewish ideas and attitudes?
- AJ writes, "It seems likely to me that Jesus did say something about the Temple," and that its destruction in 70 confirmed, for the Gospel writers, his critique. Read Jeremiah 7:1-11. AJ wonders whether Jesus's concerns about the Temple echoed Jeremiah's. What were Jeremiah's concerns? How are his concerns relevant to Christians as they worship today?
- AJ notes some Jews and Christians today "anticipate a third temple" in Jerusalem. What makes this hope, in AJ's words, "a major problem"? Do you think Christians should support calls for a third temple? Why or why not?
- "We do well," AJ suggests, "to know the history of the buildings and of the land where we worship." What do you know about your church building's history? Who built it, and was the labor voluntary or forced? Who owned its site before it was built? If worshipping in North America or Australia, which indigenous peoples owned the land where your church building now stands before European

colonization? What geographical features, if any, make the land unique or distinct? How do or how ought such issues shape your congregation's life in and use of its building and land today?

The Inscription on Jesus's Cross

Recruit a volunteer to read aloud John 19:19-22. Tell participants the sign on Jesus's cross is known as the *titulus* (TIH-choo-luss), the Latin word for "inscription." It is John's version that is recalled by most artistic depictions with the letters *I.N.R.I.*, standing for the Latin translation of "Jesus of Nazareth, King of the Jews." Discuss:

- According to AJ, the titulus indicates "Jesus dies on the charge of sedition" and warns "all passersby...this is what Rome does to any who challenge, or are perceived to be challenging, the empire." Why would Rome perceive claims about Jesus as a king as challenging its authority? Do you think Jesus challenged Rome's rule? How would you define *sedition*? How do—or should—governments today warn against or respond to sedition?
- In John's Gospel, Pilate adds Jesus's name and hometown to the titulus "to humiliate both Jesus and his fellow Jews." How does Pilate's deliberate effort to humiliate Jesus and Jesus's people affect the way you think of Pilate?
- Pilate had the titulus written in Hebrew, Latin, and Greek so as many literate people as possible could read the charges against Jesus. What theological or spiritual significance might John and early Christians have seen in Pilate's use of many languages?
- Why would "the chief priests of the Jews" feel what AJ calls "desperation" as they object to Pilate's wording of the charges? How might John 11:47-50 help answer this question?

- Read John 19:12-15. Although this episode is part of John's overwhelmingly negative depiction of "the Jews"— the name John uses throughout his Gospel for those who oppose Jesus—it also raises the question for people of faith, in AJ's words, "Who is the ultimate, rightful king? The answer 'Caesar'—or any political authority—is never the right answer." How do you determine when and whether your allegiance to a political authority compromises your allegiance to God? To what extent can congregations be politically active without crossing that line?

- AJ notes that Jesus in John's Gospel "*never claimed* to be 'King of the Jews.'" Read John 6:14-15 and 18:36-37. How and why did Jesus challenge worldly expectations of authority and those who rule? If, as AJ states, Jesus's "enthronement" in John is his crucifixion, what can Christians conclude about the true nature and purpose of power?

Closing Your Session

Read aloud the question from *Witness at the Cross*: "What do we do when we know something, sponsored by the state, or by the religious group to which we belong, is wrong?"

Ask volunteers to name things they believe the state or the church are doing are wrong. List responses on newsprint or markerboard, or on your videoconferencing platform's whiteboard. Tell participants now is not the time to disagree with or judge each other's responses; they should have those important conversations at other times. Be certain you are prepared to begin the list yourself.

Once all who wish to respond have done so, ask volunteers to describe briefly something they are doing, will do, or could do to avoid being a not-so-innocent bystander in the face of wrong. Again, be prepared to respond first.

If you think you need to adapt this activity to make participants more willing to participate, you may ask them to write their responses on paper "for their eyes only." But you may rather remind participants of AJ's challenging invitation from *Witness at the Cross*: "Nobody said this was going to be easy. As always, getting to Easter means time at the cross and time at the tomb."

Lead this prayer aloud or one of your own:

Merciful God, whenever we gloat at others' misfortune; whenever we place more faith in our buildings and our beliefs than we do in you; whenever we pledge more allegiance to our political leaders and to our nation than to you and your reign—in all these times, we confess we are there as Jesus is crucified. By your Spirit, save us from being bystanders, and make us active participants in his work of creating a heaven on earth, until that day your will is finally and fully done. Amen.

Session 2

THE OTHER VICTIMS

Session Goals

This session's readings and discussion will help participants:

- Examine their preconceptions about not only the two men crucified with Jesus but also convicted and condemned criminals today.
- Consider how Jesus's actions, teaching, and death between two other condemned men challenge ideas about greatness and power.
- Explore how the two men's words to Jesus in Luke's Gospel raise questions about criminal justice, life as good neighbors, and the present experience of paradise.
- Name and pray for people who are in various ways affected by crime and violence.

Biblical Foundations

James and John, the sons of Zebedee, came forward to [Jesus] and said to him, "Teacher, we want you to do for us whatever we ask of you." And he said to them, "What is it you want me to do for you?" And they said to him, "Grant us to sit, one at your right hand and one at your left, in your glory." But Jesus said to them, "You do not know what you are asking. Are you able to drink the cup that I drink, or be baptized with the baptism that

*I am baptized with?" They replied, "We are able." Then Jesus
said to them, "The cup that I drink you will drink; and with the
baptism with which I am baptized, you will be baptized; but to
sit at my right hand or at my left is not mine to grant, but it is
for those for whom it has been prepared."*

*When the ten heard this, they began to be angry with James and
John. So Jesus called them and said to them, "You know that
among the Gentiles those whom they recognize as their rulers
lord it over them, and their great ones are tyrants over them.
But it is not so among you; but whoever wishes to become great
among you must be your servant, and whoever wishes to be first
among you must be slave of all. For the Son of Man came not to
be served but to serve, and to give his life a ransom for many."*

Mark 10:35-45

*One of the criminals who were hanged there kept deriding him
and saying, "Are you not the Messiah? Save yourself and us!"
But the other rebuked him, saying, "Do you not fear God, since
you are under the same sentence of condemnation? And we
indeed have been condemned justly, for we are getting what we
deserve for our deeds, but this man has done nothing wrong."
Then he said, "Jesus, remember me when you come into your
kingdom." He replied, "Truly I tell you, today you will be with
me in Paradise."*

Luke 23:39-43

Before Your Session

- Read chapter 2 of *Witness at the Cross*, noting topics about
  which you want or need to do further research.
- Read this session's Biblical Foundations several times, as
  well as background information about them from trusted
  biblical commentaries and other references.
- You will need: Bibles for participants and/or on-screen slides
  to share prepared with Biblical Foundations, newsprint, and
  a markerboard.

- *Optional:* Select an image of the Crucifixion (the second of an eventual six), preferably one that depicts the two men between whom Jesus was crucified.

Starting Your Session

Welcome participants. Express your enthusiasm for leading this study of AJ Levine's *Witness at the Cross* and what you hope to gain from your group's time together. Invite volunteers to do the same.

Optional: Show participants the second of the six images of the Crucifixion you've selected.

Ask:

- What about this image most draws your attention, and why?
- *(If applicable)* Focus on this image's depiction of the two men crucified with Jesus. What thoughts and feelings does this image evoke in you?
- What do you like about this image? What do you dislike about it?

Read aloud from *Witness at the Cross:* "The Bible forces us to ask the hard questions, and it will not let us avert our eyes from sin and guilt." Tell participants this session will explore some of those "hard questions" raised by the two men who were crucified with Jesus.

Lead this prayer aloud or one of your own:

Holy God, strengthen us to stand, in our minds and hearts, before the cross of Jesus, that we may wrestle with questions asked by those crucified with him and hear in new ways his promise of paradise. Amen.

Robbers, Revolutionaries, Real Individuals

Form four groups of participants and have each turn in their Bibles to one of the four Gospel chapters depicting Jesus's crucifixion (Matthew 27, Mark 15, Luke 23, and John 19). Ask groups to compare and contrast the language used to identify the men crucified with Jesus (NRSV: "bandits" in Matthew 27:38, 44 and Mark 15:27; "criminals" in Luke 23:32, 39; "two others," John 19:18; responses may vary according to the translations participants use). Ask what thoughts, images, and feelings each word used evokes for participants. Discuss:

- AJ says the Greek word for "bandits," which Mark and Matthew use, also appears in Luke 10:30; Matthew 21:13; Matthew 26:55; John 10:1, 8; and 2 Corinthians 11:26. How, if at all, do any of these biblical echoes influence your view of the men crucified with Jesus?

- "[W]hat circumstances might drive a person to become a bandit," asks AJ, "and what circumstances might have prevented a person from committing a crime?" How would you answer? To what extent does or ought a criminal justice system consider these questions when dealing with those who commit crimes?

- AJ notes some commentators "see these two men not as robbers in the sense of someone committing a crime, but as freedom fighters or revolutionaries," partly because of what the Gospels say about Barabbas (read Matthew 27:15-17; Mark 15:6-7; Luke 23:19; John 18:40). AJ points out that "some scholars promote this connotation of rebel [because] they want to make Jesus into a . . . political revolutionary." Does considering the men crucified with Jesus as "revolutionaries" change your attitude toward or opinion about them? Why or why not?

- "One person's freedom fighter is someone else's terrorist," writes AJ. "How do we determine the correct label?" How do *you* decide which is which?

- AJ paraphrases one of her students at Riverbend Maximum Security Institute: "We are individuals, not just 'the rapist' or 'the murderer.' God-forbid that you would be known by the worst thing you ever did." How easy or difficult do you find it to think about those convicted of crimes and incarcerated as fellow human beings, created in God's image? Why? How might taking this truth about their identity more seriously change prisons in your society? What practical role do churches and other communities of faith have to play in highlighting this truth?

At Jesus's Right Hand and Left Hand

Recruit volunteers to read aloud Mark 10:35-45 (as the narrator, Jesus, James, and John (the two brothers can read in unison), and, if desired, other participants can make grumbling noises as the narrator reads verse 41!). Discuss:

- AJ imagines Jesus responding to James and John in verse 36 "with some degree of exasperation," considering their request comes immediately after Jesus has again predicted his suffering, death, and resurrection (see Mark 10:32-34). What tone of voice do you "hear" Jesus using, and why?
- Reflecting on Jesus's first question to the brothers, AJ writes, "There are numerous things we might ask for [from Jesus], if given such a blank check." What have you wanted from Jesus in the past? What do you want Jesus to do for you today? Why?
- James and John understand being at Jesus's right and left hand as positions of greatness. How is their request at odds with Jesus's teachings in Mark 8:34-37 and 9:33-37, and with the example his miracles of healing set throughout Mark 1-9?
- What are the "cup" and "baptism" to which Jesus refers? How might the brothers' assertion of their ability to drink Jesus's "cup" and receive his "baptism" anticipate Mark 14:29-31? Have you ever overestimated your ability to

follow Jesus? What happened? Have you ever found discipleship difficult? What happened?

- Why do the other disciples get angry with James and John?
- How does Jesus again, in Mark 10:42-44, challenge his disciples' assumptions about greatness? How does he connect this challenge to his own mission (verse 45), and why does this connection matter?
- Where do the disciples' assumptions about greatness surface in the world today? How do or could you and your congregation challenge these assumptions? Do you think of your church as "great"; if so, how, and if not, why not?
- How do we communicate Jesus's message about service while acknowledging the harm inflicted in slavery and other forms of forced servitude, past and present?
- As AJ notes, "two other men, dying on two other crosses" end up on Jesus's right and left (Mark 15:27). What connections can you make between this narrative detail and the story of James and John's request?

Conversation Among the Crucified

Recruit a volunteer or volunteers (as the narrator, Jesus, and the two other men) to read aloud Luke 23:39-43. Discuss:

- AJ notes verse 39, in the original Greek, says one of the men "blasphemed" Jesus. Read Luke's two other uses of this word, in 12:10 and 22:65 (NRSV "insults"). How do these three instances help us understand what "blasphemy" was for Luke?
- AJ says the man who blasphemes Jesus is speaking honestly from his pain and disappointment. "Luke gives us this glimpse into [the man's] despair… [and] invites readers to speculate: Might we be this honest in our doubts?" When was a time, if ever, you honestly voiced your own pain and

despair to God in this way? If you have not, why not? How
does your congregation voice its pain and doubts in its
worship? Have you ever prayed a lament Psalm for yourself?
Have you ever read one liturgically?

- Read Luke 4:9-13. How is the man's blasphemy another
temptation for Jesus to face? "Ironically, and sadly," AJ
writes, "a stranger"—the other man crucified with him—
"defends Jesus when his own disciples do not. Help and
support can come from the most unexpected places." When
have you received unexpected help or defense? When have
you given help to or supported someone else? How does this
man's defense of Jesus's innocence challenge prejudices and
stereotypes about people recognized to be criminals? Would
you want to be endorsed by a person convicted of a capital
crime?

- AJ states that the second man "provides a lesson in how
we can and should take responsibility for our own actions,
major or minor, that would run counter to morality." How
easy or difficult do you find it to admit when you are in the
wrong? How might this scene from Jesus's crucifixion help
you admit it in the future?

- AJ says she and her students at Riverbend take issue with
the second man's acceptance of his punishment: "No one
deserves to be tortured to death." How do we determine
whether a punishment is just or unjust? Do you think there
are some forms of punishment no one deserves? If so,
which ones? If not, why not? Can you think of appropriate
responses to criminal activity that would not require
incarceration? What role, if any, do faith communities have
in helping society determine just punishments for crime?

- "What might it mean to know," AJ asks, "that God *remembers us*, that we are not forgotten, that we matter?" When, if
ever, have you, like the second man, asked or demanded (AJ
says the man's request is both) Jesus or God to remember

you? How does or how would believing God knows, takes notice of, and remembers you make a difference to you?

- AJ suggests that when we think of paradise, "the place may be less important than the company we keep. We might shift our concern from *where* we shall live to *with whom* we shall live." If paradise is living with Jesus, how can Christians experience that life today? With whom else do Jesus's words and actions in the Gospels suggest we will live in paradise? How can we experience that life with them in this world?

Closing Your Session

Read aloud from *Witness at the Cross*: "My insider students want to be remembered. ...The call to remember is not just a plea for an afterlife marked by freedom rather than imprisonment; a call to remember is to make sure we do not treat our fellow human beings like numbers on a uniform or at a roll call, but that we treat them as individuals. A call to remember is to think about justice, in sentencing, in how prisons house and feed individuals, in what the justice system can do to help in rehabilitation, in attending to the concerns of the victims and their families, and also to the families of perpetrators."

Discuss:

- What is our congregation doing, or what could we be doing, to remember those who are imprisoned by addressing these or related issues?
- What is our congregation doing, or what could we be doing, to remember those who are victims of violence?

Lead this prayer aloud or one of your own:

Righteous God, this world falls so far short of your good will for it. Remember all people who live in the wake of crime and violence: victims, perpetrators, those imprisoned justly and unjustly, those awaiting execution, those sworn to protect the public safety and to administer justice. Remember [read names from a list of group members aloud]. Strengthen us to seek true justice and to pursue true peace, for the sake of him who was taken away by a perversion of justice, but who promises your kingdom will come and is even today present among us. Amen.

Option: Arrange for someone involved with a ministry or social service relevant to one or more of the criminal justice issues AJ highlights in this chapter to speak with your group, including about opportunities for involvement and support.

Session 3

THE SOLDIERS

Session Goals

This session's readings and discussion will help participants:

- Recognize the Gospels' distinct depictions of what Roman soldiers said and did at Jesus's crucifixion, and understand the theological and ethical significance of each depiction.
- Gain a basic familiarity of the role of centurions in the Roman Empire.
- Explore how Matthew's and Luke's accounts of Jesus healing a centurion's son or slave raise questions about power, authority, and relationships between God's people and "outsiders."
- Consider how they may respond with greater righteousness to people who are suffering.

Biblical Foundations

When [Jesus] entered Capernaum, a centurion came to him, appealing to him and saying, "Lord, my servant is lying at home paralyzed, in terrible distress." And he said to him, "I will come and cure him." The centurion answered, "Lord, I am not worthy to have you come under my roof; but only speak the word, and my servant will be healed. For I also am a man under authority, with soldiers under me; and I say to one, 'Go,' and he goes, and to another, 'Come,' and he comes, and to my slave, 'Do this,' and the slave does it." When Jesus heard him, he was amazed and said to those who followed him, "Truly I tell you, in no one in Israel have I found such faith. I tell you, many will come from east and west and will eat with Abraham and Isaac and Jacob in the kingdom of heaven, while the heirs of the kingdom will be thrown into the outer darkness, where there will be weeping and gnashing of teeth." And to the centurion Jesus said, "Go; let it be done for you according to your faith." And the servant was healed in that hour.

Matthew 8:5-13

Now when the centurion and those with him, who were keeping watch over Jesus, saw the earthquake and what took place, they were terrified and said, "Truly this man was God's Son!"

Matthew 27:54

Now when the centurion, who stood facing him, saw that in this way [Jesus] breathed his last, he said, "Truly this man was God's Son!"

Mark 15:39

When the centurion saw what had taken place, he praised God and said, "Certainly this man was innocent."

Luke 23:47

Before Your Session

- Read chapter 3 of *Witness at the Cross*, noting topics about which you want or need to do further research.
- Read this session's Biblical Foundations several times, as well as background information about them from trusted biblical commentaries and other references.
- You will need: Bibles for participants and/or on-screen slides to share prepared with Biblical Foundations, newsprint, and a markerboard.
- *Optional:* Select an image of the Crucifixion (the third of the eventual six), preferably one that depicts the soldiers and/or the centurion at Jesus's cross.

Starting Your Session

Welcome participants. Ask those who attended the previous session what they remember most from it and how it has influenced their thinking, praying, and actions.

Optional: Add the third of the six images of the Crucifixion you've selected to the display in your meeting space, and/or share the image on your screen. Ask:

- What about this image most draws your attention, and why?
- (*If applicable*) Focus on this image's depiction of the Roman solider(s). What thoughts and feelings does this aspect of the image evoke in you?
- What do you like about this image? What do you dislike about it?

Tell participants this session will explore how the Gospels' various depictions of the centurion and other soldiers at the Crucifixion raise important theological and ethical questions for people of faith today.

Lead this prayer aloud or one of your own:

Holy God, strengthen us to stand, in our minds and hearts, before the cross of Jesus, that we may learn to respond to all who suffer with greater compassion and righteousness. Amen.

The Roman Soldiers at Jesus's Cross

Form four groups of participants. Have each turn in their Bibles to one of these four passages: Matthew 27:32-37; Mark 15:21-24; Luke 23:26, 33, 36-38; John 19:23-25. Ask them to discuss the following questions and have a volunteer give a brief report to the whole group about their small group's findings. :

- How is the soldiers' treatment of Simon of Cyrene in Matthew, Mark, and Luke a display of Roman power? (For more on Simon, see the introduction to *Witness at the Cross*.)

- In all four Gospels, the soldiers throw dice for Jesus's clothes. The detail is an allusion (indirect reference) to Psalm 22:18 in Matthew and Mark and a direct reference to it in John. Why did early Christians connect this psalm to Jesus's death? What does the soldiers' gambling, in itself, reveal about their attitude toward their task?
- Why might Luke, uniquely, portray the soldiers as joining other bystanders in mocking Jesus? How is their mockery informed by Roman ideas about authority and power?
- AJ notes the centurion in Mark 15:44-45 confirms the fact of Jesus's death to Pilate. Why is this detail important for Christians' message about Jesus?
- "Roman hands crucify Jesus," writes AJ, "and Roman eyes watch him die." Why is it important for Christians today to remember the Roman Empire's responsibility for Jesus's death?
- Where today do you see the insensitivity of the powerful and privileged toward those who suffer and die, even when they are complicit in that suffering and death? When, if ever, have you acted with such insensitivity yourself?

Introducing Centurions

Ask for participants' knowledge and impressions—from their educations, Sunday school lessons, or popular culture like the "sword and sandal" movies AJ references—of Roman soldiers and centurions. Review the following information from chapter 3:

- Centurions were Roman army officers who commanded "centuries," units of 80 (not 100) soldiers, and who had administrative and judicial responsibilities.
- Centurions were elected by tribunes (military officials) in the Roman republic, and they could be appointed by the emperor once the republic became an empire.

- Centurions were "expected to be natural leaders, not head-strong but steady, not inclined to attack but ready to protect their posts at all costs."
- Centurions were usually literate, well paid, and "a number gained Roman citizenship," which carried such certain rights (see how Roman citizenship benefited Paul in Acts 22:25-29; 25:10-12).
- Rome stationed no soldiers in Galilee during Jesus's day (Herod Antipas would have had his own soldiers), though Pontius Pilate, the Roman governor of the province of Judea, which is where Jerusalem is located, "had his own troops." Rome stationed a legion of soldiers in Judea after it destroyed the Temple in 70 CE.

As time and interest allow, you might also encourage participants at computers or with smart devices to scan reputable websites about history for other information about Roman centurions.

Discuss:

- Who might we consider centurions' counterparts today and why? Do we think of high-ranking military officers today as natural leaders, "steady, not inclined to attack"? Can you name any such officers today or in the past?

Jesus Heals a Centurion's Servant

Recruit volunteers to read aloud Matthew 8:5-13 (as the narrator, the centurion, and Jesus). Discuss:

- As AJ notes, the centurion addresses Jesus, in Matthew's Greek, as *kyrios*, which "can have the connotation of 'sir' (as in 'lords and ladies'), but it is also the Greek term used to translate the Hebrew name of God, YHWH. Matthew leaves it up to the readers to determine what inflection we want to give the term." What do you think the centurion's calling Jesus "lord" indicates? What do you mean when you call Jesus "lord"?

- The person who is paralyzed in the centurion's home could also be the centurion's child; as AJ notes, the Greek word Matthew uses can mean either servant/slave or child. To what extent, if any, does this information change how you think about the centurion's request of Jesus, and why?

- AJ states the centurion's response reflects "not only the obedience but also the trust that marks the Roman military system." How closely related are obedience and trust, in your opinion, and why? The word for "faith" in Greek (*pistis*) can also mean "trust"; how do you see faith and trust as both synonymous and distinct? What qualities other than trust, if any, can motivate obedience? AJ says, "the assembly gathered in Jesus's name" should function with similar trust. When have you experienced such trust in the church?

- Does or ought obedience to human authorities also play a role in your assembly? How does this obedience differ from obedience in a military system?

- AJ claims that the centurion recognizes not only the status of those enslaved to him but also "his own status as enslaved, with only God (and not the emperor) as his master." Do you read the centurion's words this way? Do you, or should you, think of God or Jesus as your "master"? How does the language of master and slave highlight virtues of faith (see Mark 10:43-44)?

- How did Jesus, as AJ says, take on the "role of one enslaved" in his life and death (see Mark 10:45; Matthew 26:42; John 5:19, 30)? How helpful or desirable is the metaphor of God as a slave master?

- Why is Jesus "amazed" (Matthew 8:10) by the centurion's response? Does Jesus's statement diminish or dismiss those in Israel who have, previously in Matthew, shown faith in him (4:24-25; 8:1-4)? What, if anything, distinguishes the centurion's faith from theirs?

- What does this amazement at the centurion lead Jesus to say about the relationship of "outsiders" (who come "from east and west") and "insiders" ("the heirs") at the future messianic feast (verses 11-12)? How does AJ say this scene anticipates the reactions of "insiders" and "outsiders" at Jesus's crucifixion?

- Read Luke 7:2-10, which is another version of the narrative in Matthew 8:5-13. Do you prefer one version of this story over the other? Why or why not? How might the elders' words (Luke 7:4) reflect complicated relationships between people who are in power and those over whom they have power? Does the centurion's physical absence from Luke's story heighten, diminish, or have no effect on his expression of faith in Jesus? How?

The Centurion's Declaration

Recruit three volunteers. Have each read aloud a Gospel account of the centurion's declaration when Jesus dies: Matthew 27:54; Mark 15:39; Luke 23:47. Ask participants what similarities and differences they notice. Discuss:

- AJ notes that some readers see Mark's centurion as being "facetious" and unknowingly ironic in calling Jesus "God's Son." How does reading the centurion's words as flippant sarcasm reinforce the conflict between human and heavenly ideas about power and authority? How comfortable or uncomfortable does this reading make you, and why? How does Matthew's added detail of the earthquake affect this reading?

- AJ also suggests Mark and Matthew's centurion "gets the point" about Jesus that his disciples do not: "Jesus's primary

role is not to be seen in the miracles." Have you known or
known of non-Christians who seem to "get" Jesus more than
many Christians do? Who and how? When and how, if ever,
have non-Christians or Christians of other denominations or
communions deepened and enriched your own faith? How
could this reading shape (or reshape) Christian evangelism?

- In Luke, the centurion refers to Jesus not as God's Son—
  since, as AJ points out, for Luke "*all* people are children of
  God" (Luke 3:38)—but as an "innocent" or, more accurately
  translated, a "righteous" man. AJ says "righteous" means
  "uprightness of character, fidelity to Torah, generosity to
  others.... a lifetime of good works." She suggests it evokes
  Isaiah 53:11b, among other Scriptures. Why might Luke
  choose to emphasize Jesus's righteousness at the cross?
  Why might he choose to have the centurion, as Rome's
  representative, do so? Had you been at the cross, witnessing
  what the centurion witnessed, what single statement might
  you have made, and why?

- AJ notes Christians through the centuries have often
  admired, told legends about, and even revered as a saint
  the centurion. Is your opinion of the centurion positive,
  negative, or neutral, and why?

Closing Your Session

Read aloud from *Witness at the Cross*: "I have my doubts that
there was a centurion at the foot of the cross.... But the words the
Evangelists place on [the centurion's] lips ring true on so many levels."
Discuss these questions inspired by AJ's reflections:

- To what extent do or ought the centurion's words help
  define what Christians mean when they refer to Jesus as
  "Son of God"?

- What ethical consequences follow from reading the centurion's statement in Matthew and Mark as an affirmation of all people as God's children?
- In Luke, AJ states, the soldier's "remind us that innocent people...are sometimes executed." What role do or should people of faith play in identifying and preventing such situations, and responding when they do occur?
- How do people of faith keep righteousness from becoming *self*-righteousness?
- How does or how could you and your congregation respond to people who suffer with increased righteousness—that is, uprightness of character, fidelity to God's commandments, and generous, good works?

Lead this prayer aloud or one of your own:

Sovereign God, you alone have the right to make an ultimate claim on our lives. By your grace and your Spirit, lead us, as those under your authority, to respond to those who suffer with greater righteousness, that we may truly know ourselves your children: merciful as you are merciful, holy as you are holy. Amen.

Session 4

THE BELOVED DISCIPLE

Session Goals

This session's readings and discussion will help participants:

- Consider how the anonymity of the "Beloved Disciple" in John's Gospel opens the possibility for any and all of Jesus's followers to be his Beloved Disciples.
- Understand how the Beloved Disciple exemplifies obedience to Jesus's "new commandment" to love.
- Explore the rumors about the Beloved Disciple's fate as invitations to consider their own testimonies to Jesus.
- Identify practical actions of loving discipleship they are taking or could take to keep "sacred time" in their and others' lives.

Biblical Foundations

After saying this Jesus was troubled in spirit, and declared, "Very truly, I tell you, one of you will betray me." The disciples looked at one another, uncertain of whom he was speaking. One of his disciples—the one whom Jesus loved—was reclining next to him; Simon Peter therefore motioned to him to ask Jesus of whom he was speaking. So while reclining next to Jesus, he asked him, "Lord, who is it?" Jesus answered, "It is the one to whom I give this piece of bread when I have dipped it in the

dish." So when he had dipped the piece of bread, he gave it to
Judas son of Simon Iscariot. . . .

[Jesus said,] "Little children, I am with you only a little longer.
You will look for me; and as I said to the Jews so now I say to
you, 'Where I am going, you cannot come.' I give you a new
commandment, that you love one another. Just as I have loved
you, you also should love one another. By this everyone will
know that you are my disciples, if you have love for one another."

John 13:21-26, 33-35

Peter turned and saw the disciple whom Jesus loved following
them; he was the one who had reclined next to Jesus at the
supper and had said, "Lord, who is it that is going to betray
you?" When Peter saw him, he said to Jesus, "Lord, what about
him?" Jesus said to him, "If it is my will that he remain until I
come, what is that to you? Follow me!" So the rumor spread in
the community that this disciple would not die. Yet Jesus did not
say to him that he would not die, but, "If it is my will that he
remain until I come, what is that to you?"

This is the disciple who is testifying to these things and has
written them, and we know that his testimony is true.

John 21:20-24

Meanwhile, standing near the cross of Jesus were his mother,
and his mother's sister, Mary the wife of Clopas, and Mary
Magdalene. When Jesus saw his mother and the disciple whom
he loved standing beside her, he said to his mother, "Woman,
here is your son." Then he said to the disciple, "Here is your
mother." And from that hour the disciple took her into his
own home.

John 19:25b-27

Before Your Session

- Read chapter 4 of *Witness at the Cross*, noting topics about
  which you want or need to do further research.

43

- Read this session's Biblical Foundations several times, as well as background information about them from trusted biblical commentaries and other references.
- You will need: Bibles for participants and/or on-screen slides to share prepared with Biblical Foundations, newsprint, and a markerboard.
- *Optional:* Select an image of the Crucifixion (the fourth of the eventual six), preferably one that depicts the Beloved Disciple and Jesus's mother at Jesus's cross.

Starting Your Session

Welcome participants. Ask those who attended the previous session what they remember most from it and how it has influenced their thinking, praying, and actions.

Optional: Add the fourth of the six images of the Crucifixion you've selected to the display in your meeting space, and/or share the image on your screen. Ask:

- What about this image most draws your attention, and why?
- (*If applicable*) Focus on this image's depiction of the man and woman standing at Jesus's cross. Who are they? What thoughts and feelings does this aspect of the image evoke in you?
- What do you like about this image? What do you dislike about it?

Tell participants this session will explore John's account of Jesus's words from his cross to his Beloved Disciple, the Disciple's response, and the relationship of the Disciple's place at the cross to his other appearances in the Fourth Gospel.

Lead this prayer aloud or one of your own:

Holy God, strengthen us to stand, in our minds and hearts, before the cross of Jesus, that we may be seen by his loving eyes and in turn see others the same way. Amen.

Who Was (or Is) Jesus's Beloved Disciple?

Read aloud from *Witness at the Cross* AJ's initial "annoyance" at the mention of the Disciple whom Jesus loved: "What are the other disciples, chopped liver? Isn't Jesus supposed to love everyone?...Jesus plays favorites?" Ask participants: "Have John the Evangelist's mentions of a particular 'Beloved Disciple' ever annoyed or confused you? Why or why not?"

Discuss:

- AJ mentions some potential "Beloved Disciple" candidates that Bible scholars and readers have identified, including: John the son of Zebedee, the purported author of the Fourth Gospel; Lazarus (on the basis of John 11:5, 36); Mary Magdalene (because of her faithfulness to Jesus and "the greater likelihood of a male versus a female author gaining an audience"). What do you think of these options? Are you aware of others?
- AJ also mentions the Beloved Disciple might be "a composite figure representing who any disciple could be or should be." How helpful do you find this possibility, and why?
- AJ points out the Beloved Disciples' ultimate anonymity focuses our attention on how he is remembered, and asks, "[I]f our names were unknown, by what titles or descriptions would we want to be remembered?" How do you answer AJ's question?

The Beloved Disciple at Table with Jesus

Recruit a volunteer or volunteers to read aloud John 13:21-26, 33-34. Discuss:

- "Although he may have been with Jesus since the calling of the first disciples," AJ points out, Jesus's last meal with his disciples before his death is the scene in which John first explicitly mentions the Beloved Disciple. Why do you think this might be? Do you remember where and when you met your closest friends? Does the setting matter?

- John's Greek in verse 25 literally says the Beloved Disciple was reclining on Jesus's breast, "a position of intimacy" (compare Abraham's bosom, Luke 16:23 ; see footnote to verse), as AJ highlights. She states some English translations "suggest an embarrassment with male friendship and male bodies in proximity." How would you assess our culture's comfort with intimate male friendships, and why? How might pointing to Jesus and the Beloved Disciple as a model of such a friendship help men today? How might seeing the Beloved Disciple as a woman change your reading of the Last Supper or the Crucifixion?

- Was there ever a time you felt particularly close to Jesus, as if you were leaning on him? Do you think of your relationship with Jesus as "intimate"? Why or why not?

- Commenting on Jesus's commandment in verse 34, AJ writes, "There is nothing new about the commandment to love one another" (see, for example, Leviticus 19:18, 34). Why does Jesus call his commandment a new one? How does he love his disciples (see also John 13:1)? What does Jesus say will result from his disciples obeying this commandment?

- Jesus tells his disciples that where he goes they cannot follow; but, as AJ suggests, obeying his commandment does mean they "can live as Jesus would have wanted [them] to live." Who are some of Jesus's "Beloved Disciples" you believe are living or lived as Jesus wanted? Why?

The Beloved Disciple's Fate

Recruit a volunteer or volunteers to read aloud John 21:20-24. Discuss:

- This episode occurs after the risen Jesus appears to some of his disciples by the Sea of Tiberias. The Beloved Disciple recognizes Jesus first (21:7). What might this detail tell us about the Beloved Disciple? Do you have your own image of what the risen Jesus looks like? How do or can we more readily recognize the risen Jesus in the world and in our lives?

- Why do you think Peter asks Jesus about the Beloved Disciple (verses 20-21)? How, if at all, might Peter's discussion with Jesus immediately prior (21:15-19) relate to his question? Why do you think the Evangelist reminds readers of the first explicit mention of the Beloved Disciple at this point?

- Why did the early followers of Jesus whom John knew and/ or for and to whom he wrote his Gospel believe the Beloved Disciple would not die before Jesus returned? What wisdom, if any, does this case study in "rumor" offer us today as we seek to understand and interpret Jesus's words and teachings?

The Beloved Disciple at Jesus's Cross

Recruit a volunteer to read aloud John 19:25b-27. Discuss:

- Unlike the disciples in Matthew and Mark, and closer than the disciples in Luke, the Beloved Disciple, with the women, "stayed the course and remained at the cross." How do or can Jesus's Beloved Disciples today stay near Jesus's cross? Do you imagine yourself at the cross or at a distance? How does your image of Jesus change as you move from one location to another?

- "There's a comfort to being seen through Jesus's eyes," writes AJ, "and there's a blessing to know that we are seen doing what we should be doing in terms of caring for those who love us." When, if ever, have you felt Jesus has seen you caring for those who love you, or for others who are in need of care? How can you and your congregation further develop "sight" like Jesus's sight, noticing and supporting caregivers?

- By entrusting his own mother to the Beloved Disciple and presenting the Beloved Disciple to her as her son, Jesus is "setting up a new family" based on his commandment in John 13:34, states AJ. How is a community based on Jesus's commandment to love one another like and unlike a family based on biology, marriage, or adoption? How does or should it differ from other "families" we choose for ourselves or in which we find ourselves?

- To what extent does or should Jesus's "new family" confirm and/or challenge how society today understands family? When are you most and least likely to think of your faith community as your family? Why?

- AJ points out that the love Jesus commands, which the Beloved Disciple here shows by taking Jesus's mother into his home, is "a practical stance, an action." In what practical, active ways does your congregation love each other?

- How can and do congregations prevent the image and language of "being a family" from becoming exclusionary? What practical, inclusive actions of love does your congregation regularly take toward those who aren't "members of the family"?

- Speaking of Jesus's mother's and the Beloved Disciple's new relationship to each other, AJ discusses how the living cannot replace the dead but can console each other. What are the most helpful and healing ways your congregation has supported someone whose loved ones have died?

Closing Your Session

Remind participants that, as AJ notes, the Fourth Gospel's final reference to Jesus's "hour" of exaltation and glory is the "hour" the Beloved Disciple takes Jesus's mother into his home. Read aloud from *Witness at the Cross*: "[E]ven time can be sacralized. Any hour can be the time when discipleship is recognized in love. The next time someone asks you, 'What time is it?' and you see the hour, these verses from John might echo in your mind. If they do, you've moved from clock time to sacred time."

Invite participants to draw a large, circular clockface on scrap paper. Ask them to write notes about or simply sketch acts of loving discipleship they perform, or could perform, at several hours of the day. Encourage them to think about where they usually are at a given hour, with whom they are immediately in relationship, and how they could take practical action for another's good. Challenge them to write or draw at least three actions—for the morning, afternoon, and evening, or one for each hour Jesus hung on his cross. Assure participants they need not show or talk about their completed clockfaces with anyone unless they wish to do so.

Lead this prayer aloud or one of your own:

Loving God, we would all be Jesus's Beloved Disciples. So grant us, in your grace, the willingness to stay close to him, even at his cross; to ask the questions he alone can answer; and to care for those he entrusts to us, both within and without his new family. Amen.

Session 5

THE WOMEN

Session Goals

This session's readings and discussion will help participants:

- Discuss the role of women as patrons of Jesus and the early church and make connections to women's contributions as leaders in and supporters of faith communities today.
- Distinguish between the four Gospels' accounts of women who witnessed Jesus's death and appreciate each narrative's distinct emphases and implications for faithful living today.
- Identify and celebrate women who have borne faithful witness to God.

Biblical Foundations

Soon afterwards [Jesus] went on through cities and villages, proclaiming and bringing the good news of the kingdom of God. The twelve were with him, as well as some women who had been cured of evil spirits and infirmities: Mary, called Magdalene, from whom seven demons had gone out, and Joanna, the wife of Herod's steward Chuza, and Susanna, and many others, who provided for them out of their resources.

Luke 8:1-3

A great number of the people followed [Jesus], and among them were women who were beating their breasts and wailing for him. But Jesus turned to them and said, "Daughters of Jerusalem, do

*not weep for me, but weep for yourselves and for your children.
For the days are surely coming when they will say, 'Blessed are
the barren, and the wombs that never bore, and the breasts that
never nursed.' Then they will begin to say to the mountains, 'Fall
on us'; and to the hills, 'Cover us.' For if they do this when the
wood is green, what will happen when it is dry?"*

Luke 23:27-31

Before Your Session

- Read chapter 5 of *Witness at the Cross* and note topics about
  which you want or need to do further research.
- Read this session's Biblical Foundations several times, as
  well as background information about them from trusted
  biblical commentaries and other references.
- You will need: Bibles for participants and/or on-screen slides
  to share prepared with Biblical Foundations, newsprint, and
  a markerboard.
- *Optional:* Select an image of the Crucifixion (the fifth of the
  eventual six), preferably one that depicts women watching
  Jesus's crucifixion.

Starting Your Session

Welcome participants. Ask those who attended the previous session what they remember most from it and how it has influenced
their thinking, praying, and actions. You might, for example, ask them
what time it is, to see if the "hour" has become sacred.

Optional: Add the fifth of the six images of the Crucifixion you've
selected to the display in your meeting space, and/or share the image
on your screen. Ask:

- What about this image most draws your attention, and why?
- *(If applicable)* Focus on this image's depiction of the women
  witnessing Jesus's crucifixion. What thoughts and feelings
  does this aspect of the image evoke in you?

- What do you like about this image? What do you dislike about it?

Tell participants this session will explore how the Gospels' accounts of the women who watched Jesus die can inspire and instruct our own discipleship today.

Lead this prayer aloud or one of your own:

Holy God, strengthen us to stand, in our minds and hearts, before the cross of Jesus, that the women who witnessed his death and bore the first witness to his resurrection may teach us how to bear faithful witness to him today. Amen.

The Women Who Supported Jesus

Recruit a volunteer to read aloud Luke 8:1-3. Discuss:

- What does Luke tell us about these women, and why?
- These women were patrons, "people with resources provid[ing] support for teachers and healers." How did women patrons continue to play important roles in the early church (see Acts 9:36-41; 16:13-15). Do you think women's patronage of Jesus and his early followers is as well known as it should be? Why or why not?
- Do you think that patrons or donors should have input into how the recipients of their patronage act?
- "Luke may be encouraging women who read the Gospel," write AJ, "to act as these women did, and so to contribute financially to the upkeep of the community without seeking leadership roles." What formal leadership roles can and do women occupy in your faith tradition? Does your congregation welcome and seek out women to fill these roles? Why or why not? Who are women in your congregation who are leaders despite not holding official roles and titles?

The Women Who Witness in Mark

Have participants turn in their Bibles to and read Mark 15:40-41. Discuss:

- Who are the women watching Jesus die? What does Mark tell us about them and their relationships to Jesus?
- Why might these women be "looking on from a distance" (verse 40)? "The women's placement, and the lack of explanation for it," suggests AJ, "serves to interrogate our own behaviors at such moments." At what moments in your life can you recall looking on suffering from a distance, and why? At which of those moments could or should you have placed yourself differently? When did you last draw close to someone who was suffering, and for what reason?
- What do these women intend to do in 16:1-3? Why does AJ think the incident narrated in 14:3-9 poses a "problem" to their plan? Do you think the earlier story reflects poorly on the women now? Why or why not?
- Do you agree with AJ that the women's worries in 16:3 make them appear "inept"? Why or why not?
- If, as AJ and most scholars agree, Mark originally ended at 16:8, what conclusions do you draw about these women's faith and faithfulness, and why?
- How do these "three named women" mirror their "three male counterparts, equally named and equally having failed"—Peter, James, and John (read 14:33-41, 72)? How do the announcement of Jesus's resurrection and the existence of Mark's Gospel itself both witness to the fact that neither the men's nor the women's failures meant the end of Jesus's story?

The Women Who Witness in Matthew

Have participants turn in their Bibles to and read Matthew 27:55-56. Discuss:

- Who are the women watching Jesus die? What does Matthew tell us about them and their relationships to Jesus?
- Read Matthew 20:20-23 (and compare Mark 10:35-40; see also session 1). Why do you think Matthew records "Mrs. Zebedee," as AJ calls her, making this request on her sons' behalf? What might we infer or imagine about her from this request? How does her request ironically anticipate the scene at the Crucifixion (27:38)?
- Why do the two Marys go to Jesus's tomb in 28:1? How does their response to the news of Jesus's resurrection in 28:8 differ from their counterparts' reaction in Mark 16? How meaningful do you find these differences, and why?

The Women Who Witness in Luke

Have participants turn in their Bibles to and read Luke 23:27-31 (you may also wish to recruit a volunteer to read it aloud). Discuss:

- Jesus calls the women along the Via Dolorosa (the route along which Jesus carried his cross) "daughters of Jerusalem," a phrase AJ points out is found elsewhere in Scripture only in the Song of Songs (Song of Solomon). "The language may be erotic," she writes, "but in antiquity, erotic language could be used to express deep theological yearnings." Do you find it appropriate, weird, or inappropriate to use erotic language when speaking of theology? How is the romantic, erotic love between human beings expressed in the Song of Songs like and unlike love between human beings and God?
- "Jesus loves the city" of Jerusalem, states AJ. How do his sayings in Luke 13:31-35 reflect this love?
- While beating one's breast was a conventional gesture of mourning in Jesus's society, AJ thinks these women could be lamenting not only an innocent man's death but also "the

miscarriage of justice and, behind it, the power of Rome." How do or how could you and your congregation publicly lament and protest miscarried justice today? How do or how could you add to your lamenting and protest other actions to effect change?

- "Jesus tells these women that their lamentation is misplaced" because Luke, in telling Jesus's story, interprets Rome's destruction of Jerusalem and the Temple in 70 CE, at the end of the First Jewish Revolt (66-70), as "a direct result of the people's failure to recognize Jesus as their lord" (read also 19:41-44). How is Luke's explanation a blaming of victims and, in AJ's words, "a disservice to history"? Can you think of a time when the recognition of Jesus as Lord led to peace rather than war between nations?

- AJ suggests Jesus's words to the women can provoke us to consider "what we can tolerate, and what we find so intolerable that we rise up in rebellion." What have you and your congregation found—or what do you think you would find—"so intolerable" you would "rebel" in some way against authority, regardless of the consequences? How do we know when, if ever, such rebellion is not only permissible but faithful?

- Who watches Jesus die in Luke 23:48-49? What does Luke tell us about these people and their relationships to Jesus?

- How is Luke's account of the women's trip to Jesus's tomb (24:1-12) like and unlike Mark's and Matthew's? What do you make of these similarities and differences?

- Luke's delay in naming some of the women who went to the tomb until after they report to "the eleven" male disciples who disbelieve them (24:9-11) suggests to AJ "that for Luke, these women are *not* apostles." How, if ever, have you seen or experienced churches minimizing or denying women's importance as leaders and contributors? What did you do (or are you doing) about it?

The Women Who Witness in John

Have participants turn in their Bibles and read John 19:25b-27. Discuss:

- Who are the women watching Jesus die? What does John tell us about them and their relationships to Jesus?
- AJ notes only John's Gospel explicitly locates Jesus's mother at his cross. "To refer to Mary as 'the mother of Jesus,'" writes AJ, "insists on his fully human embeddedness, in biology and in relationship." Why does John insist on Jesus's humanity (see also 1:14)? How might Jesus's consistent address of his mother as "Woman" (see also 2:4) reinforce this insistence?
- In calling his mother "Woman," says AJ, Jesus "retains her identity apart from being a mother." To what extent do you think our society views women who are mothers as *only* or primarily as mothers? What does or might your church do to challenge such a view, without denying or devaluing mothers' importance?
- AJ notes other women whom Jesus, in John, addresses as "Woman." Read about these women in 4:21; 8:10; 20:15 (and these verses' surrounding context). What connections can you make between these women and the woman who witnesses her son's death?
- Do you think that maternal love is different from paternal love? If so, how so?

Closing Your Session

Read aloud from *Witness at the Cross*: "The women at the cross have been ignored or reduced to models of simple piety. . . . When Jesus states, 'Woman!' he is not restricting his conversation partner to a gender role; he is making sure she is noticed."

Invite volunteers to talk briefly about particular women they know or have known who have been important to their faith as:

- women who were patrons (literally or figuratively) of the congregation, or of the participant personally;
- women in formal or informal leadership roles;
- women who provided maternal or sisterly love and loyalty, regardless of biology;
- women who spoke truth to them in unexpected ways;
- women who lamented and protested injustice, or rebelled against authority or the status quo in a faithful way;
- women who in some other way bore witness to God or Jesus.

Write these women's names on newsprint or markerboard, or on your videoconferencing platform's whiteboard, and incorporate them into your closing prayer.

Lead this prayer aloud or one of your own:

O God, source of life: We praise you for the women who have borne witness to you in myriad ways [including...]. May their examples inspire us, also, to testify to your truth, act in faithfulness, and reach out to others in love. Amen.

Session 6

JOSEPH OF ARIMATHEA AND NICODEMUS

Session Goals

This session's readings and discussion will help participants:

- Compare and contrast the four Gospels' depictions of Joseph of Arimathea, considering the implications each portrait of Joseph carries for their own beliefs and actions.
- Explore Nicodemus as a model of a sympathizer to Jesus who does not become his disciple and how faith communities should engage with such sympathizers today.
- Reflect on their experience of this study and how it has changed not only their views of the witnesses to Jesus's crucifixion but also their own responses to Jesus and to the Gospels that tell his story.

Biblical Foundations

When evening had come, and since it was the day of Preparation, that is, the day before the sabbath, Joseph of Arimathea, a respected member of the council, who was also himself waiting expectantly for the kingdom of God, went boldly to Pilate and asked for the body of Jesus. Then Pilate wondered if he were already dead; and summoning the centurion, he asked him whether he had been dead for some time. When he learned from the centurion that he was dead, he granted the body to Joseph. Then Joseph bought a linen cloth, and taking down the body, wrapped it in the linen cloth, and laid it in a tomb that had been hewn out of the rock. He then rolled a stone against the door of the tomb.

Mark 15:42-46

After these things, Joseph of Arimathea, who was a disciple of Jesus, though a secret one because of his fear of the Jews, asked Pilate to let him take away the body of Jesus. Pilate gave him permission; so he came and removed his body. Nicodemus, who had at first come to Jesus by night, also came, bringing a mixture of myrrh and aloes, weighing about a hundred pounds. They took the body of Jesus and wrapped it with the spices in linen cloths, according to the burial custom of the Jews. Now there was a garden in the place where he was crucified, and in the garden there was a new tomb in which no one had ever been laid. And so, because it was the Jewish day of Preparation, and the tomb was nearby, they laid Jesus there.

John 19:38-42

Before Your Session

Read chapter 6 of *Witness at the Cross*, noting topics about which you want or need to do further research.

Read this session's Biblical Foundations several times, as well as background information about them from trusted biblical commentaries and other references.

You will need: Bibles for participants and/or on-screen slides to share prepared with Biblical Foundations, newsprint, and a marker-board.

- *Optional*: Select an image of the Crucifixion (the sixth and last), and/or images of the burial of Jesus's body or Nicodemus talking with Jesus at night.

Starting Your Session

Welcome participants. Ask those who attended the previous session what they remember most from it and how it has influenced their thinking, praying, and actions.

Optional: Add the sixth of the six images of the Crucifixion or the image of Jesus's burial or Nicodemus's visit to Jesus that you've selected to the display in your meeting space, and/or share the image on your screen. Ask:

- What about this image most draws your attention, and why?
- What thoughts and feelings does this image evoke for you?
- What do you like about this image? What do you dislike about it?

Tell participants this session will explore how the Gospels' accounts of Joseph of Arimathea and Nicodemus's involvement with Jesus during his ministry and trial, and in the burial of his body, raise questions for us about the extent of our own commitment to what we believe is right.

Lead this prayer aloud or one of your own:

Holy God, strengthen us to stand, in our minds and hearts, before the cross of Jesus, that we may discover, as did Joseph of Arimathea and Nicodemus, the points at which you call us to commit ourselves to righteous action for the sake of your coming kingdom. Amen.

Spinning Joseph of Arimathea's Story

Form four groups of participants. Assign to each group one of the following Scriptures: Mark 15:42-46; Matthew 27:57-60; Luke 23:50-54; John 19:38-42. Ask each group to make a list of everything their assigned Scripture states about Joseph of Arimathea. After allowing a few minutes for groups to complete this assignment, have each one report its findings. Start with the Mark group, listing their responses on newsprint, markerboard, or videoconference whiteboard. Then proceed through the Matthew, Luke, and John groups' responses, adding check marks when details are repeated and writing new details as needed.

Tell participants this activity reveals something of what AJ calls the "spin control" in which the Evangelists appear to have engaged as they retold Joseph of Arimathea's involvement in Jesus's death and burial. Read aloud from *Witness at the Cross*: AJ does not think "concluding a biblical passage might be more spin control than fact, or parable rather than history, is necessarily a bad thing.... Not everything needs to have happened, in the sense of being caught on a camera, in order to be meaningful." Discuss:

- Read Mark 14:55-65. Why does Mark's characterization of Jesus's trial before the Sanhedrin (the highest Jewish court in Roman-occupied Judea) make his account of Joseph's request for Jesus's body surprising?
- Mark states Joseph was waiting for God's kingdom (15:43). "To wait for the kingdom and *not* to act on that desire is to fail to act in partnership with God," writes AJ. How does Joseph's request demonstrate his desire to partner with God? In what specific ways are you and your congregation partnering with God as you anticipate the full coming of the Kingdom?
- Joseph's ownership of a tomb in Jerusalem "would be a sign of reverence, but it could also be a sign of some economic security," and Matthew explicitly calls Joseph rich. What do you want your burial arrangements to show those who survive you about your status and values?
- Because Matthew doesn't mention Joseph earlier and, like Mark, characterizes the Sanhedrin's treatment of Jesus as cruel, AJ wonders whether Matthew identifies Joseph as a disciple to "entice" readers, "perhaps especially well-off readers," to "learn more" about Jesus. Why might Matthew have felt well-off readers needed a disciple with whom they

could identify? (See also 19:23-24, Matthew's only other use of the word *rich*.)

- AJ says Joseph "continues to look better and better" in Luke 23:50-53. What questions does Joseph's stated righteousness raise about his role in Jesus's trial before the Sanhedrin? Whatever Joseph did or didn't do, when have you found yourself wanting or needing to speak against a group to which you belong? What did you do? What happened?
- Why do you think Luke doesn't identify Joseph as rich? (See also 12:16-21; 16:19-31; 19:8-9).

Getting to Know Nicodemus

Recruit a volunteer to read aloud John 19:38-42. Discuss:

- John mentions Nicodemus's nighttime visit to Jesus. Read or skim Jesus and Nicodemus's conversation in John 3 and identify the ways Nicodemus is "figuratively in the dark" as well as literally. What symbolic significance do darkness and light, as well as day and night, carry in John's Gospel (see 1:4-9; 8:12; 9:4; 11:9-10; 13:30)? How do these associations influence your attitude toward Nicodemus?
- Nicodemus acknowledges Jesus's signs (3:2), but AJ notes she has known people who say the signs Jesus performs in John "make them depressed rather than inspired." Why can stories of signs and miracles in Scripture present difficulties for faith today? If a faith based on signs is, as AJ writes, "a faith based on the wrong details," why does John devote attention to Jesus's signs? AJ suggests we can see other kinds of "signs" in the world and in our lives—what are they, and what do they signify?
- As Nicodemus's misunderstanding of the comments Jesus makes regarding being born from above illustrates, "Jesus is not always clear." Why does John depict Jesus as not

always speaking plainly (but see also 11:14; 16:29-30)? Do you think faith in Jesus must involve ambiguity and risk misunderstanding? If so, how much? If not, why not? How might having to work your way through difficult material make the results more meaningful?

- Read Nicodemus's second appearance, in John 7:45-52. "Once again," writes AJ, "Nicodemus does the right thing, and once again he does not become a disciple." How does this episode shape your opinion of Nicodemus, and why?

- "For me," writes AJ, "Nicodemus represents the sympathizer" to the church or synagogue who attends and is involved "but who is not technically a member." How well (or poorly) does your faith community welcome its "Nicodemuses"? Have you ever been a "Nicodemus" in a faith community, or are you one now? How can faith communities do more to ensure their "Nicodemuses" are "welcomed, cherished, and treated with love"?

- AJ explains that caring for the dead is, in Judaism, an "entirely altruistic" fulfillment of a *mitzvah* (God's command) because "there is no possibility of reciprocation.... The corpse is not going to return the favor." How does your congregation care for the dead, and for the living the dead leave behind?

God and Nature

AJ observes the roles that God and nature play as additional witnesses at the cross. Consider the following questions:

- AJ notes that the presence of God is made manifest through "the tearing of the Temple veil, the darkness, the earthquake, and the raising of the saints." How are each of these depicted in the Crucifixion scene? How do you interpret them?

- "The heavens were opened, God mourned, and nature, too, mourned." What does it mean for God to mourn? How do you see God as active during this excruciating moment?
- AJ concludes, "God and nature remain, but we all come away from the cross changed in some way." How are you changed by the stories of the witnesses at the cross?

Closing Your Session

Remind participants this is your group's final session studying *Witness at the Cross*. Thank group members for their participation, and express your gratitude for being able to facilitate the study.

Read aloud from the conclusion of *Witness at the Cross*: "I see the witnesses at the cross first as figures we all might try on.... [W]e readers do well to listen to their stories and see how their stories transform us. At that point, we pick up the story ourselves."

Discuss (you will likely want to write these questions ahead of time and display them for participants to choose from, rather than ask every group member to respond to each one):

- During the course of our study, which witness at the cross did you find most engaging or attractive, and why?
- Which witness did you find most challenging to read and talk about, and why?
- Which witness's role might you "try on" in your own prayers and actions, and why?

Lead this prayer aloud or one of your own:

High and holy God, Jesus said that when he was lifted up, he would draw the whole world to himself. May we, who have been drawn to his cross through our study together, now go to the world you so love, carrying with us a keener vision for those who suffer, a stronger commitment to justice and peace, and a resolve to live in righteousness, that the new life Jesus promises may be evident in our lives. Amen.

.

Made in the USA
Middletown, DE
17 February 2023

25029445R00036